Charleston's
SIGNATURE SIPS ®

The subtropical climate in the Lowcountry makes cold drinks a necessity here, and while porches seem ideal for sipping, you really should get out every now and then. Whether you like craft beer, PBR, vintage wines, cheap hooch, or fancy cocktails, there's a bar in Charleston for you.

About the Author

Steven W. Siler is a firefighter-cum-chef serving in Charleston, South Carolina. He is the author of several cookbooks of restaurant recipes from across the nation. In addition, he has served as an editor and contributing writer for several food publications.

The Restaurants

Prohibition	Dewberry Hotel	The Windjammer
FIG	Market Pavilion	The Ordinary
Cocktail Club	McCrady's Tavern	The Blind Tiger
The Bar at Husk	O-Ku	Zero George
Stars	Fiery Ron's Home	Restaurant + Bar
Tavern & Table	Team	Old Village Post
Rooftop at	Hall's Chophouse	House
Vendue	The Vintage	High Cotton
MacIntosh	Proof	Warehouse
HōM	Bar Mash	The Grocery
The Rarebit	Thoroughbred Club	Locals
Pavilion Bar	Edmund's Oast	Hank's
Voodoo	39 Rue de Jean	The Gin Joint

Experience the *Signature Tastes* from around the world!

Take your tastebuds for a stroll through Charleston's restaurants!

Charleston CULINARY TOURS

www.SignatureTastes.com
(206) 222-2048

www.CharlestonCulinaryTours.com
(843) 259-2966

Old Fashioned

The story starts in Louisville, Kentucky in 1880. A private social club, called The Pendennis Club, is credited for making the very first old-fashioned. James E. Pepper, bartender and esteemed bourbon aristocrat, invented the drink in Louisville, before he brought the recipe to the Waldorf-Astoria Hotel bar in New York City. Fast forward to 1936 where an old-timer describes the cocktail in the New York Times. "Time was...the affable and sympathetic bartender moisted a lump of sugar with Angostura bitter, dropped in a lump of ice, neither too large or too small, stuck in a miniature bar spoon and passed the glass to the client with a bottle of good bourbon from which said client was privileged to pour his own drink."

Yup, the whole bottle. Oh how the times have changed!

Recipe

One of the hottest cocktail bars in Charleston, Prohibition takes a modern approach to old school booze: the house specialty is a bacon-maple Old Fashioned, and there's distinctly Southern palette in drinks like the King Street Cobbler (blackberry brandy, lemon, muddled sugar, and brandy-infused berries in a rocks glass)

For the Bacon Infusion:
3 or 4 slices bacon, or enough to render 1 ounce of fat. Prohibition uses Benton's, but any extra-smoky variety will do) (1) 750-ml. bottle of bourbon such as Four Roses Yellow Label

For the Cocktail:
2 oz. bacon-infused bourbon
¼ oz. Grade B maple syrup
2 dashes Angostura bitters
Twist of orange

For The Bacon-Infused Bourbon:
Cook bacon in pan and reserve rendered fat. When bacon fat has cooled a bit, pour off one ounce from pan. Pour bourbon into a non-porous container. Strain the bacon fat into the container and infuse for 4 to 6 hours at room temperature. Place mixture in freezer until all the fat is solidified. With a slotted spoon, remove fat and strain mixture back into bottle.

For The Cocktail:
In mixing glass, stir 2 ounces bacon-infused bourbon, maple syrup, and bitters with ice. Strain into chilled rocks glass filled with ice. Garnish with orange twist.

{ *"Happiness is having a rare steak, a bottle of whisky, and a dog to eat the rare steak."*
Johnny Carson }

Sazerac

Although it's not the most widely known drink, the Sazerac is both delicious and one of America's oldest cocktails. The blend of rye whiskey, bitters, sugar, and absinthe or pastis dates all the way back to the 1830s when Creole pharmacist Antoine Peychaud came up with the recipe and began serving it. The Sazerac became so popular that Peychaud's apothecary business quickly became better known as a place to get a revitalizing potion. The Sazerac is currently in the middle of something of a resurgence. Kentucky distillery Buffalo Trace has marketed two very good straight rye whiskeys under the Sazerac name, and last year the Louisiana House of Representatives proclaimed that the drink is the official cocktail of New Orleans.

Recipe

Before every young chef wanted to move to Charleston to open a restaurant, there was FIG. The name is an acronym for "Food Is Good," a simple epithet that doesn't do justice to the level of cooking set forth by Mike Lata, the godfather of Charleston restaurants, and yet sums it up completely.

1 cube sugar	Pack an Old-Fashioned glass with ice
1½ oz. Sazerac Rye Whiskey or Buffalo Trace Bourbon	In a second Old-Fashioned glass place the sugar cube and add the Peychaud's Bitters to it, then crush the sugar cube
¼ oz. Herbsaint	
3 dashes Peychaud's Bitters	Add the Sazerac Rye Whiskey or Buffalo Trace Bourbon
Lemon peel	to the second glass containing the Peychaud's Bitters and sugar
	Empty the ice from the first glass and coat the glass with the Herbsaint, then discard the remaining Herbsaint
	Empty the whiskey/bitters/sugar mixture from the second glass into the first glass and garnish with lemon peel

{ *"Where's your sense of adventure?" he asks Bond, ordering him a Sazerac. "This is New Orleans. Relax!"*
Felix Leiter to James Bond in
To Live and Let Die }

La Raza

Recipe

This is one of Ryan Welliver's (from the Cocktail Club) favorite cocktails named the La Raza (Spanish for "the race". The name is taken from the Spanish name for Columbus Day in South America, "dia de las razas". It is also served it during the Cooper River Bridge Runs.

2oz Casa Noble Blanco Tequila
1 oz. lime juice
½ oz. House Falernum**
½ oz. Vanilla syrup

Falernum:
Wrey & Nephew Jamaican Rum -2 liters
6 pods of star anise
12 pods of cloves
3 Tbsp Allspice Berries
2 drops of almond oil
2 stalks of lemongrass
1 cup of pistachio milk (extracted from milking 1 cup of pistachio nuts)
6 zests of a lime
3 zests of a lemon
juice of 3 lemons
juice of 3 limes
1 cup of shredded ginger
2½ cups of demerara sugar
5 cups filtered water

Toasted Pistachio Milk:
1 cup pistachios
2 cups warm water

For The Cocktail:
Shake all the ingredients with ice. Strain into chilled cocktail glass. Garnish with dehydrated lime wheel.

For the House Falernum:
1. Begin by making Pistachio milk.Then, in a separate mixing bowl, pour 2 bottles of overproof rum.
2. Add cloves, star anise,allspice, almond oil and lemon & lime zests to rum. Then allow this to sit uncovered at room temperature for at least 24 hours also.
3. Add the pistachio milk to mixing bowl. Next, add lemon juice, lime juice and almond oil. Then, chop ginger and lemongrass stalks and add to bowl. Put all ingredients into a blender. Pulse on high for 30 seconds. Meanwhile, boil 5 cups water with the Demerara sugar to create a simple syrup. Lastly, combine all ingredients.
4. Strain all through a chinois.
If using sous vide/immersion circulator technique, combine all ingredients except water and sugar into large mason jar. Set immersion circulator to 135 degrees Fahrenheit. Place mason jar into the water bath and cook for 4hrs agitating occasionally. Remove from bath, and transfer mixture to the blender. Blend at pulse on high for 30 seconds. Strain thoroughly. Make syrup from the sugar and water, combine the two mixtures.Store in refrigerator for up 2 months.

Toasted Pistachio Milk:
In a large, dry saucepan, toast the pistachios over medium-low heat, stirring constantly, until golden brown. Transfer to a blender and add the water. Pulse until the pistachios are finely chopped, then blend for 1 minute. Strain through large coffee filter lined sieve.

Charleston Light Dragoon's Punch

The story of the Charleston Light Dragoons is interwoven with the social and military history of South Carolina from early colonial days. The corps existed at least as early as 1733, being called then with British loyalty the "Charleston Horse-Guards," a title changed at the Revolution into "Charleston Light Dragoons. There are two references to Charleston Light Dragoon punch in only two 'old cookbooks,' Charleston Receipts from 1950 and a 1908 oddity with the succinct title Famous Old Recipes Used a Hundred Years and More in the Kitchens of the North and South Contributed by the Descendants, "compiled by" Jacqueline Harrison Smith. Smith calls her formula 'Dragoon Punch,' but leaves no doubt that we are dealing with the drink drunk by the Charleston mounted militia:

"This punch is known as Dragoon punch, and has been made by Mr. Louis F. Sloan, of Charleston, for the last 50 years, for the Charleston Light Dragoons, and has become famous…. and this is the first time it has ever been in print."

Recipe

The Bar at Husk, an off-shoot of James Beard Award-winning Chef Sean Brock concept, Husk, prepares a modern interpretation of this that is one of the bar's most popular cocktails.

4 cups raw sugar
3 cups fresh lemon juice from about 24 lemons
4 quarts black tea
4 quarts California brandy
1 quart Bermuda or Barbados rum
½ pint peach brandy
Peels of 6 lemons, cut into slivers
1½ quarts soda water

Combine sugar, lemon juice, tea, brandy, rum, peach brandy, and lemon peels in a large bowl. Stir until sugar is dissolved and chill in refrigerator for at least 1 hour.

Add ice (preferably in one large block) and top with soda water before serving. Alternatively, top each glass with 1 ounce of soda water before serving.

Storm the Beach

The history of Tiki drinks can be traced back to the 1930s, when a man named Don Beach opened the first Tiki bar in Hollywood, California. Don was inspired by the Polynesian culture that he had experienced while travelling in the South Pacific. To recreate the flavors that he experienced in Hawaii, Don mixed rum with fresh fruits, such as pineapple and guava.

By the 1950s, airline travel had made the Hawaiian Islands more accessible to visitors from all over the globe. During the 1950s and 60s, Hawaiian culture became very popular in movies and magazines. Tiki bars started to appear all over the United States, signalizing the rise of this cultural trend.

Recipe

Cockktail Club's Ryan Welliver won the 2017 Charleston Wine + Food Rum Rum Rudolph Cocktail Competition. Ryan's Storm the Beach Tiki Cocktail was selected to be the official cocktail for Charleston Wine + Food 2017 and was also featured in Imbibe Magazine.

Cinnamon-Cumin Syrup:
1 cup water
2 cups white sugar
2 cinnamon sticks
1 Tbsp. ground cumin seed

For the Cocktail:
1 oz. Hamilton 86 Demerara Rum
½ oz. Plantation O.F.T.D
½ oz. Velvet Falernum
½ oz. fresh grapefruit juice
½ oz. fresh lime juice
½ oz. cinnamon-cumin syrup
2 drops Bittermens Elamakule Tiki Bitters

For the Cinnamon-Cumin Syrup:
Toast the cumin until fragrant. Grind into a course powder. Set aside. Bring the cinnamon and water to a boil in a medium-sized saucepan. Boil for 10 minutes. Turn off the heat. Add the sugar and cumin. Stir until the sugar has dissolved. Allow the syrup to cool to room temperature. Strain through a fine-mesh strainer. Bottle and refrigerate for up to 2 weeks.

For The Cocktail:
Shake all the ingredients with ice. Strain in a glass filled with crushed ice. Garnish with a grapefruit slice.

{ *"Anyone who says I didn't create this drink is a dirty stinker."*
Vic Bergeron on the Mai Tai cocktail }

Dixon Daquiri

Following the American Victory in the Spanish-American War, the U.S. moved into Cuba to capitalize on the rich Cuban iron mines with Jennings Cox, working for the Baltimore-based Bethlehem Steel leading one of the first expeditions into the Sierra Maestra mountains close to the town of Daiquiri . One night, while entertaining guests from the mainland, Cox ran out of Gin but thankfully, due to generous rations, he had built up quite a stash of the local Bacardi Carta Blanca rum. So as not to expose the delicate constitutions of his guests to straight rum, Cox mixed it with lime juice and sugar, thus creating the Daiquiri. In 1909, the USS Minnesota was touring the now decade-old battlegrounds of the Spanish American War. Captain Charles H. Harlow went ashore at Guantanamo with then junior medical officer Lucius Johnson in tow. The duo soon met up with none other than Jennings Cox, who was more than happy to share his creation with them. Johnson was instantly smitten with the drink. Returning to the United States with a stash of Cuban rum and Jenning's recipe, Johnson soon instructed the bar staff at Washington D.C.'s Army and Navy Club on how to prepare his new favorite cocktail. The Daiquiri was such a hit that the bar (now named the Daiquiri Lounge) sports a plaque to honor of the moment.

Recipe

This love child of a daquiri and a margarita cocktail gets its name from Heather Dixon of Stars Restaurant, now Greene after her recent marriage. A huge thanks to Budd Huber from a galaxy far away at Calhoun Corners (Go Tigers!) for this recipe.

1½ oz. Espolon Tequila
½ oz. Luxardo Maraschino liquor
1½ oz. grapefruit juice
½ oz. fresh grapefruit juice
½ oz. simple syrup
½ oz. lime juice
micro-cilantro

Shake all ingredients with ice and double strain into a cocktail glass. Garnish with additional micro-cilantro.

{
"This frozen daiquiri, so well beaten as it is, looks like the sea where the wave falls away from the bow of a ship when she is doing thirty knots."
Islands in the Stream *by Ernerst Hemingway*
}

THE BEST
Wine BARS

A restaurant that happens to have a list of wines by the glass is not a wine bar, no matter what they say on the sign outside. A wine shop that has a little tasting area where they sometimes pour wines for customers to taste doesn't qualify either. A wine bar is a haven created by passion for wine, a cozy place to enjoy it, and unbridled knowledge that begs to be shared with patrons.

O'HARA & FLYNN
225 Meeting St.
··········

Located just steps from the Belmond Charleston Place, this little nook looks like a library, but the shelves are filled with wine. On weekends, you're apt to find more locals because it's when they host live jazz, which makes this place even more charming.

AVONDALE WINE & CHEESE
813-B Savannah Hwy.
··········

This cute West Ashley shop features a great selection of cheese and wine, along with regular wine tastings hosted by gracious shopkeep Manoli Davani.Manoli has tapped into something great with her store: nothing less than the rebirth of good local shopping.

BIN 152
152 King St.
··········

As much as I'd love to keep this place a secret, I can't....this is one of my favorite places in Charleston to have a drink. From the antiques and art on the walls, to the window seats and lack of pretension...did I mention charcuterie, cheese and chocolates?

ARDOA WINE BAR
1960 Riviera Dr. Mt P
··········

Ardoa is modern French and offers great food selections such as cheeses, charcuterie, paté, foie gras, rillettes, and desserts. The kicker is a self-serve wine dispenser; just push a button and you can taste a wide variety of wine, where you decide the depth of pour.

ELLIOTBOROUGH MINI BAR
18 Percy St.
··········

As one customer put it, EMB is like "being in a cooler version of your own living room. I love the music, the artwork, and the overall worn in feel of the place."
And don't let the size fool you: "...And though she be but little, she is fierce!"

WINE & COMPANY
441 Meeting St., Ste B
··········

Owner Joshua Walker describes Wine & Company as a cross between Debbie Marlowe's Wine Shop and Bin 152, meaning customers can drink wine onsite or buy bottles to take home. No formal servers means no pressure to leave; i.e. means stay and sip.

Paloma

According to the Oxford English Dictionary, moonshine is defined as "whisky or other strong alcoholic drinks made and sold illegally." With that definition, it may be confusing to walk into liquor stores (or Costco) and find booze labeled as moonshine.

Part of the problem lies in the lack of federal requirements for labeling something as moonshine. Unlike whiskey, which must be made from grain, distilled and bottled at a certain alcohol content, and aged in oak, 'shine has no equivalent. Like vodka, it can be made from anything fermentable: fruit, sugar, grain, or milk. Like vodka, there's no upper limit on its alcohol content. Unless you want to describe it as white whiskey on the label, you can make it any way you please. So, despite what you might have read in the OED, legally made hooch labeled "moonshine" is all over the place.

Despite its super Southern connotation, hooch isn't exclusively a Southern drink. The term moonshine has been around since the late 15th century, but it was first used to refer to liquor in the 18th century in England. Back then, whiskey was even used in some places as currency.

Recipe

Like neighborhood taverns of old, Tavern & Table on Shem Creek is designed to be that local gathering place where friends and family get together for classic cocktails and spectacular handcrafted food in an atmosphere as comfortable as your living room.

1 cube sugar
1¼ oz. Belle Isle Honey
Habanero Moonshine
¾ oz. grapefuit juice
¼ oz. lime juice
¼ oz. honey syrup
3 oz. San Pelligrino
Blood Orange soda

Shake all the ingredients except soda with ice. Strain in a glass filled with ice. Finish with the blood orange soda. Garnish with a grapefruit slice.

{ *We are here and it is now. Further than that, all human knowledge is moonshine.* *H. L. Mencken* }

Pimm's Cup

The tawny-colored gin-based liquor Pimm's No. 1 Cup is the foundation of the eponymous cocktail. In the 1840s James Pimm, the exalted landlord of an oyster bar in London's financial district, invented and marketed it as a health tonic. The mixture became so popular over the next decade that Pimm then began selling his top-secret concoction commercially and then globally as the fingers of the British Empire reached into India, Canada, Australia and the Caribbean.

Recipe

The Rooftop at Vendue sits above the self-styled "Charleston's Art Hotel," so everything from the tile floors to the artwork on the wall is impeccably decorated. The rooftop was remodeled a couple of years ago, now offering views of the French Quarter and the Charleston harbor,

1½ oz. Pimm's No. 1	Add the soda to a Fizz or Collins glass and set aside.
1 oz. cucumber puree, strained	Add the remaining ingredients to a shaker and shake without ice for about 10 seconds. Add 3 or 4 ice cubes
½ oz. St. Germain	and shake very well. Strain into the prepared glass.
2 oz. Sanpellegrino Limonata	Garnish with a cucumber slice and lemon twist.

{
"... I feel sure you will enjoy yourselves there, for the bartender has the secret of a remarkable gin fizz, sweeter than a maiden's smile, more intoxicating than a kiss."
Rex Beach, in his 1911 novel
The Ne'er-Do-Well
}

Witchdoctor

The Szechuan button (also known as the electric daisy or buzz button) grows on a species of herb called Acmella oleracea. When consumed, it releases a naturally occurring alkaloid that produces a strong numbing or tingling sensation in the mouth, followed by excessive salivation and then a cooling feeling in the throat. It gives a whole new meaning to the word "mouthfeel". What's more, as the tingling and numbing sensations gradually wear off, the drink's flavors and temperature seem to change with every sip. In essence, for a short amount of time, everyone becomes a supertaster.

Recipe

The Macintosh, on upper King Street, is where Executive Chef Jeremiah Bacon, a three-time James Beard semifinalist, merges his exceptional technique-driven fare with locally sourced ingredients for a modern American experience. The Witchdoctor is their award-winning cocktail.

1½ Hendricks Gin Cucumber Mint 1 cube sugar ½ oz. St. Germain Elderflower liquer Szechuan button	Pack an Old-Fashioned glass with ice. In a second Old-Fashioned glass place the sugar cube and add cucumber and mint to it. Muddle well. Add the Hendrick's gin and St. Germain to the glass with ice and shake, along with the muddled cucumber and mint. Strain into a martini glass, and top with the Szechuan button.

{ The Szechuan button used to be used in old-timey dentist's offices to numb a patient's mouth, so it offers a slight numbing sensation that'll leave you singing all night long! }

Bloody Mary

Around 1920, émigrés escaping the Russian Revolution began arriving in Paris, bringing with them vodka and caviar, where Harry's, a New York bar dismantled and reassembled in Paris, awaited them. Harry's bartender, Ferdinand "Pete" Petiot, began experimenting with the new Russian spirit, which he found tasteless. At the same time Petiot was introduced to American canned tomato juice, which back in the dry days of Prohibition was called a "tomato juice cocktail" on menus. Petiot continued at it until a new cocktail was born, called the Bucket of Blood, christened by visiting American entertainer Roy Barton after a West Side Chicago nightclub of the same name.

Recipe

Bloody Mary's, along with their ever-present sidekick the Mimosa, form a potent Sunday duo in Charleston. And few do it better than HōM, anchoring the burger scene on Upper King Street. Robbie George has created a layered, smokey version guaranteed to chase hangover blues away.

1½ oz. bacon-infused vodka
Bloody Mary mix
1 celery stalk, for garnish
1 lemon slice, for garnish
1 lime slice, for garnish
1 strip cooked bacon, for garnish

Bacon-Vodka Infusion:
1 750 mL bottle vodka
12 slices thick-cut bacon
1 1/3 Tbs. organic maple syrup

HoM Bloody Mary Mix:
1 46 oz. can of V8 juice
1/3 cup Worcestershire sauce
1 1/3 Tbs. Tabasco sauce
¼ C. A1 Steak Sauce
¼C. KC Masterpiece BBQ Sauce
1 1/3 Tbs. horseradish
1/3 Tbs. celery salt
¼ C. Guinness
1 1/3 Tbs. lemon juice
2 Tbs. salt
2 tsp. pepper

Fill a pint glass with ice. Add bacon-infused vodka. Fill rest of glass with Bloody Mary mix. Top glass with shaker and shake well. Garnish with celery stalk, lemon and lime slices on rim, and strip of bacon. Serve.

Bacon-Vodka Infusion:
Cook bacon in a fryer and put in a container, glass preferably. Add maple syrup over bacon. Pour vodka over syrup and bacon. Seal container with an airtight lid and let sit for five days at room temperature..Strain vodka into an empty bottle as many times as necessary to remove larger pieces of fat. Use a cheesecloth to remove remaining fat. Store in a cooler or at room temperature.

HoM Bloody Mary Mix:
Combine all ingredients, stir, and store in a sealable container. Refrigerate for five to seven days.

Moscow Mule

In 1941, Sophie Berezinski was a woman on a mission. She had immigrated to the United States from Russia and was carrying a heavy burden: 2,000 solid copper mugs. She and her father had owned the Moscow Copper Co in Russia, and had designed and stamped the iconic cup. Under pressure by her husband Max to get the mugs out of their house, Sophie went door-to-door trying to sell them. Stopping at the famous Cock 'n' Bull pub on the Sunset Strip, Sophie happened on the owner, Jack Morgan, and his good friend John Martin, owner of the then-floundering Smirnoff distillery. Sensing an opportunity, they put their heads together and created the now-iconic cocktail, in it's signature copper mug.

Recipe

With a long marble-topped bar, fresh seafoam green paint, and green-and-black plaid seats on the booths, the Rarebit is a retro-styled King Street diner captures the feel of the pre-Hippie '60s. This version is their signature cocktail.

2 ounces Pinnacle vodka
5-7 ounces Sweatman's ginger beer
1 ounce limeade
lime zest
lots of crushed ice
copper mugs

Rinse copper mugs with cold water and fill ⅔rds of the way full with crushed ice. Pour the vodka over ice. Add limeade. Add ginger beer and garnish with lime zest. Serve immediately.

Limeade:
Boil down a 5-to-1 ratio of fresh lime juice to agave syrup.

{ *Once we hit forty, women only have about four taste buds left: one for vodka, one for wine, one for cheese, and one for chocolate.*
Gina Barreca }

Pavilion Punch

As Charleston was once home to the opulent Planter's Hotel, and the city's trading proximity to tropical islands that produce rum, it's widely believed that Planter's Punch originated here. "Charleston's famed Planter's Punch was first introduced here," declares the online history of the Dock Street Theater, rebuilt on the site of the once-grand hotel."Planter's Punch goes back to the 1830s, maybe even earlier," Southern food chronicler Eugene Walter wrote in a collection of cocktail recipes, "It started out as first-quality rum blended with lemon or lime juice, but now there are literally hundreds of versions."

Recipe

The Pavilion Bar, sitting atop the Market Pavilion hotel, offers year round outdoor drinking and dining, with incomparable views of the Cooper River and Charleston Harbor. Even better, is drinking this refreshing punch whilst dancing on top of the plexiglass-topped pool at night.

1½ oz. Myers dark rum 2 oz. cranberry juice 2. oz. pineapple juice 2.oz. orange juice splash of grenadine	Pour the ingredients into a mixing glass filled with ice cubes. Shake well. Strain into a highball glass filled with ice cubes. Top with club soda if you want. Garnish with seasonal fruits.

{ *Planter's Punch became hugely popular in America in the postwar period. When film siren and native Southern Belle Tallulah Bankhead died in 1968, Time Magazine remembered, "she was known to romp around her apartment in the nude drinking Planter's Punch."* }

Mai Tai

The Mai Tai may be Polynesian in name, but it's American in origin, created not on a tropical lagoon but on the mudflats of San Franciso's East Bay in 1944, by a legendary California restaurateur, the late Vic Bergeron of Trader Vic's fame.

The Mai Tai became popular at Trader Vic's restaurants in Oakland, San Francisco and Seattle. In 1953, Bergeron introduced the Mai Tai to Hawaii at the Royal Hawaiian and Moana Hotels whose well-heeled guests arrived by Matson Line steamships.

By the 1980s, the original version of the Mai Tai could be found in Waikiki only at the Halekulani, which takes great pride in serving classic cocktails by original recipes. New York bartender Danny DePamphillis reintroduced the original Mai Tai at the Moana Hotel in 1986. It was perfect-Trader Vic would have been proud.

Recipe

The Avondale restaurant Voodoo brings some much-needed counterculture vibes to the Lowcountry, with a few velvet paintings and wild full moon parties thrown in the mix. Dimly lit with garish red and black, it's a perfect escape with the original Mai Tai.

1 oz. light rum
1 oz. dark rum
1 oz. fresh lime juice
½ oz. orange curacao
3/4 oz. Voodoo Falernum
Lime shell and mint sprig for garnish

Voodoo Falernum:
8 oz overproof rum (such as Wray and Nephew or Lemon Hart 151)
50 cloves
10 limes, zested
1 cup julienne ginger
simple syrup

Pour the ingredients into a cocktail shaker filled with about 2 cups of crushed ice. Shake well. Pour everything (do not strain) into an old-fashioned glass. Garnish with a lime shell sunk into the ice and a sprig of fresh mint.

Voodoo Falernum:
Toast the cloves over medium heat until they are fragrant, about 5 minutes shaking the pan being careful not to burn them. Drop the cloves and remaining ingredients into the rum. Cover with plastic wrap, or a tight lidded jar and let steep for 24 to 48 hours. After 48 hours strain through a coffee filter. Add steeped mixture to a 2:1 simple syrup

Panic Button

Like so many cocktails, the origins of the Manhattan are lost in time. The Democrat newspaper remarked in 1882 that, "It is but a short time ago that a mixture of whiskey, vermouth and bitters came into vogue" and observed that it had been known as a Turf Club cocktail, a Jockey Club cocktail and a Manhattan cocktail. Some now think that a man going by the name of 'Black' invented the cocktail at the famed Hoffman House in New York City. Whichever story you choose to believe The Manhattan Club still lays claim to the ownership of the recipe to this very day and the cocktail is still widely available in bars, restaurants and cafes throughout the world and is regarded by many bartenders as one of the best cocktails to ever have been served.

Recipe

The Dewberry Hotel's iteration of the classic Manhattan uses Averna and Campari. Produced in Sicily since the 19th century, both are one of many Italian liqueurs known as amari. They range from light and sweet to profoundly bitter, but have a few things in common: They're generally consumed as an aperitivo before dinner to kick up the appetite, or a digestivo afterwards. And since they're made according to proprietary recipes, steeped with roots, herbs, and more, each one is unique.

1½ oz. bourbon
¾ oz. Averna
½ oz. Campari
½ oz. Heering cherry liqueur
¼ oz. fresh lemon juice

Shake all the ingredients with ice to chill, then strain into a glass holding a single large ball or cube of ice.

{
"Ho! Ho! Ho! To the bottle I go
To heal my heart and drown my woe
Rain may fall, and wind may blow
And many miles be still to go
But under a tall tree will I lie
And let the clouds go sailing by"
J.R.R. Tolkien
}

THE BEST *Dive* BARS

The term dive bar entered the lexicon in the 19th century as a way to describe a bar or opium den that was literally subterranean. There's a folk etymology as well—going in meant you were headed out of sight and into a zone of ill repute. The main activity that takes place there has to be drinking. No karaoke, definitely no bar trivia. A TV can be there, but it should be old, unremarkable, and probably tuned to the local news.

RICHARD'S
2237 N. Hwy 17, Mt. P
• • • • • • • • • •

There's nothing fancy or frilly at Richard's. The place is dimly-lit, covered in stapled-up dollar bills signed by patrons, and decorated with Confederate battle flags, casting nets, and movie stills. And there is always a couple of Harleys parked in the front.

GENE'S HAUFBRAU
817 Savannah Hwy.
• • • • • • • • • •

Billing itself as "Charleston's oldest bar, by far, Gene's anchors the Avondale drinking scene, especially after midnight. Spacious yet dark, with obligatory pool tables, and a sheltered, outdoor patio for the equally obligatory Marlboro after a hard day's work.

UPPER DECK TAVERN
353 King St.
• • • • • • • • • •

Upper Deck Tavern (UDT) is the type of place that's intimidating at first — there's no sign, you have to travel down a dark alley, and the stairwell to the bar can leave you second guessing your every step. It's a shot and beer bar with PBR in every variation.

SALTY MIKE'S
17 Lockwood Dr.
• • • • • • • • • •

Skid row used to refer to the seedy waterfront areas of most coastal cities. Charleston was no different. There are few things finer than a dark 'n' stormy sipped over a sunset on the deck at Salty Mike's. A mix of sailors, blue collar workers, and businessmen, all with a little larceny in the heart.

MOE'S CROSSTOWN
714 Rutledge Ave
• • • • • • • • • •

Moe's Crosstown Tavern has one of the most loyal followings of any dive bar in town. It's also one of the few you'll find with a packed house at lunch and dinner and on gameday. Even their Sunday brunch is packed, no doubt due to the appropiately named "Drunken French Toast".

RECOVERY ROOM
685 King St.
• • • • • • • • • •

There's nothing about the Recovery Room Tavern that can't be said about any other dive bar under any other overpass in America. It's a windowless hovel with pinball, pool, and foosball. But astonishingly, it is also the #1 seller of Pabst Blue Ribbon cans in the world.

Champagne Nitrotini

Many historians follow the martini back to a miner who struck gold in California during the Gold Rush. The story goes that a miner walked into a bar and asked for a special drink to celebrate his new fortune. The bartender threw together what he had on hand — fortified wine (vermouth) and gin, and a few other goodies — and called it a Martinez, after the town in which the bar was located. The Martinez was a hit, and word soon spread about the new drink. It was published in the Bartender's Manual in the 1880s. The current name of "martini" may have gotten its name because of Martini & Rossi vermouth, says Robert Hess, secretary of the Museum of the American Cocktail in New York. A customer asks for a 'Martini' cocktail because it utilized that product, much as they might ask for a 'sherry' cocktail in those days if they wanted a cocktail which used sherry. During the 1800s, many drinks were named very simply (gin cocktail, fancy gin cocktail, gin cobbler, gin daisy, etc.)

Recipe

Cooled to -320 Fahrenheit, the Nitrotini is Charleston's only cocktail infused with liquid nitrogen. Dramatic, sexy and delicious, the Nitrotini is possibly the coldest and most refreshing cocktail you have ever tasted, and is available only at the Market Pavilion Hotel bar.

1½ oz. Pomegranate schnapps	Pour the ingredients into a mixing glass
1 oz. Cointreau orange liqueur	filled with ice cubes. Shake well. Strain into
3 oz. Louis Perdrier Champagne	a martini glass. Top with liquid nitrogen,
orange slice to garnish	and enjoy once the vapors have stopped.

{ *"Drinking with skill and taste is no more a natural art than love; either it must be learned by the onerous process of trial and error, or it must be taught"*
H.L. Mencken }

McCrady's Cobbler

The instigator for the exploration of Madeira was Enrique el Navegador. He himself traveled to Madeira and in 1450 he decided that there had to be viticulture on there. The first vines came from Crete: the grapes that are still in production today were "Malvasia Candida". Madeira wine was used as ballast for the sailing ships through their journeys to India and South America. The long journey in the warm tropical climate simmered the wine slowly. Every wine gets totally damaged by this process, but Madeira wine only benefits from it. Charelston, being a sea port on the Atlantic, was a popular destination for sailors arriving from Europe, and consequently the tasty ballasts of Madeira wine.

Recipe

In 1778, Edward McCrady built a four-story Georgian house on East Bay Street and opened McCrady's Tavern. Today, McCrady's Tavern is pure Sean Brock, a multi-James Beard winner whose creative-obsessive culinary tinkering catapults classic dishes into an otherworldly sphere of decadent comfort.

1½ oz. Broadbent Rainwater Madeira
1½ oz. Lustau Amontillado Sherry
Shaved Ice
Orange
1 Tbsp. Caster Sugar
blackberries

Pour the alcoho and sugar into a cocktail shaker filled with about 2 cups of crushed ice. Shake well. Pour everything (do not strain) into an copper mug filled with shaved ice. Garnish with an orange slice, berries on a stick and a sprig of fresh mint.

{ *The Amontillado sherry in this cocktail is a nod to Edgar Allen Poe, a once-residence of Fort Moutrie on Sullivan's Island, and author of The Cask of Amontillado* }

Yuzu Crazy

By the early 1800s, sushi had become something of a fast food in Tokyo; chef Hanaya Yohei is generally regarded as having invented "modern-style" sushi at this time, although his fish was generally marinated in soy sauce or lightly cooked to prevent spoilage. Inexpensive sushi stands proliferated, and when they were outlawed by the government because of sanitation issues, the chefs took to opening restaurants instead.

ushi finally made its way across the Pacific in 1966, when Noritoshi Kanai and business partner Harry Wolff opened Kawafuku in Los Angeles' Little Tokyo. It was a huge success with Japanese businessmen, who introduced sushi to their American colleagues. Four years later, Osho opened in Hollywood and became popular with celebrities and other movers and shakers.

Recipe

O-Ku, of the Indigo Road restaurant family, has set the standard for sushi in Charleston. This cocktail, along with several other signature libations on the menu, come courtesy of the Shinto priestess of aperitifs, Bar Manager Allison Radecker.

2 oz. Toki japanese whiskey ½ oz. averna ½ oz. Aperol 1 oz. yuzu juice	Pour the ingredients into a mixing glass filled with ice cubes. Shake well. Strain into a martini glass.

{ *"Whiskey, like a beautiful woman, demands appreciation. You gaze first, then it's time to drink."*
Haruki Murakami
Japanese bestselling author }

Game Changer

A version of the classic Pusser's Painkiller® had its start at the six-seat Soggy Dollar Bar on a long stretch of white sand beach at White Bay on the island of Jost Van Dyke in the British Virgin Islands. There's no dock, so the usual way in is to swim. Of course, your dollars get wet, hence the name "Soggy Dollar Bar."

It was owned by an English lady, Daphne Henderson. Boaters, including Pusser's founder, Charles Tobias, came from distant places to sample her version of the Painkiller for which she'd become locally famous. Tobias had gone to The Admiralty Board of the Royal Navy and gained permission to commercialize the rum in 1979 made him curious about this deliciously concocted recipe made with Pusser's Rum. He then reverse-engineered the cocktail to it's modern derivation.

Recipe

Fiery Ron's Home Team BBQ keeps machines full of this frozen elixer spinning all year round. As Pusser's Rum owns the trademark to the name "Painkiller", Home Team has their version known as the Game Changer. And so it is, being the signature cocktail on Sullivan's Island, lovingly offered by the incomparable Jessie White.

2 oz. spiced rum
4 oz. pineapple juice
1 oz. orange juice
1 oz. cream of coconut
Crushed ice
Fresh grated nutmeg

Add liquid ingredients to a cocktail shaker and shake vigorously. Pour into a blender and puree until smooth. Pour into a big glass. Grate fresh nutmeg on top and enjoy!

{ *Daphne Henderson and Charles Tobias became good friends, but in spite of their close friendship, and no matter how he tried, she refused to divulge her secret recipe for the Cocktail. He managed to get one through the surf into his boat to take home.* }

Hummingbird

Our modern steakhouse has two direct ancestors, the beefsteak banquet and the chophouse. Both arose, interestingly enough, in mid-19th century New York City, a town that got the best beef cuts the country had to offer because only there did diners have enough money to pay for them. They got their name from what was served: sliced beef tenderloin, each piece placed upon a slice of white bread like an open faced sandwich. The bread slices, however, were rarely eaten and were mainly stacked besides each plate as an informal scorekeeping system for how much beef was consumed by the participants. The Old Homestead of New York served its first charcoal broiled strip just after the Civil War, in 1868. In fact, a surprising number of steakhouses that opened around the same time are still open today: Keens and the Palm chain in Manhattan and the legendary Peter Luger in Brooklyn are all going strong today.

Recipe

Hall's Chophouse is the premier steakhouse experience in Charleston, hearkening back to the glory years of perfect steaks, strong cocktails and flawless service. The Hummingbird is Hall's most-requested signature cocktail.

1½ oz. Cathead Honeysuckle Vodka
1 oz. Lillet Blanc
½ oz. Cointreau
½ oz. lime juice

Pour the ingredients into a mixing glass filled with ice cubes. Shake well. Strain into a martini glass.

{ *Most bereaved souls crave nourishment more tangible than prayers: they want a steak.*
M. F. K. Fisher }

Toast and Marmalade

The story goes that marmalade was invented in 1700, when a storm-damaged Spanish ship, carrying Seville oranges, sought refuge in Dundee harbour. The cargo was sold off cheaply to James Keiller, a down-on-his-luck local merchant, whose wife turned it into a preserve. Winston Churchill steeled himself for war with it (washed down in the morning with a flute of Pol Roger), D H Lawrence wrote novels on it, Paddington Bear would put nothing else in his sandwiches. Yet the origins of the stuff are mysterious, and Britain's claim to have invented it surprisingly shaky. The Romans were partial to a gooey fruit preserve, usually made from quinces preserved and sweetened by honey, which was known as "marmelo". The name and its derivations are found all over Europe – "marmelada" in Greece, "marmelatta" in Italy. It began arriving at the Port of London in the late 15th century. It was greatly sought after, but far from slapping it on a morning slice of toast, the fashionably gentry would serve it as a sweet at the end of a meal.

Recipe

Inspired by the tried-and-true combo of jam on toast, this brunch cocktail from he MacIntosh's Megan Deschaine perfectly translates breakfast to the cocktail glass.

1½ oz. bourbon
¼ oz. Drambuie
½ oz. honey syrup
½ oz. fresh lemon juice
1 heaping barspoon orange marmalade
2 dashes Bittermen's Mole bitters

Shake all the ingredients well, pour the contents into a double rocks glass. Garnish with thyme sprig and an orange slice

{ *"Here's to alcohol, the rose colored glasses of life."*
F. Scott Fitzgerald
The Beautiful and Damned }

N.Y. Sour

The recipe for the Sour was first written down in the 1862 book <u>The Bartender's Guide</u> by Jerry Thomas. However, the basic recipe was known for over a century prior. In those days, travel seemed to take forever, and up to the 20th century, refrigeration was lacking and the concept of germs was largely unknown. Long journeys over land weren't terrible. You could stop off and resupply as needed or just go hunting and foraging. Sea travel, especially from Europe to North America, was not nearly as simple. Food and water will spoil over a multi-month trip, and water wasn't exactly considered safe.

Professional sailors suffered from scurvy and other malnutrition and sea-sicknesses, up until a bartender's hero named Vice Admiral Edward Vernon of England began mixing a few ingredients together to serve to his crew. Sailors had a ration of various things, like limes and lemons to prevent scurvy, and liquor for something safe to drink. To prevent a ship full of intoxicated shipmates, the liquor, usually rum once it was discovered, was watered down and lemon or lime juice was added to mask the flavor of the rum. Hence, we have a very early version of the Sour.

Recipe

The Vintage's Nathan Wheeler is masterfully recreating and updating both classic cocktails, as well as exploring new directions for the pleasure of patron's of this King Street stalwart.

2 oz. bourbon	Add all ingredients excpet wine to a shaker without ice.
1 oz. simple syrup (1:1, sugar:water)	Shake vigorously for 30 seconds.
1 oz. lemon juice	Strain into a cocktail glass with one large cube.
Carmiere wine or other full-body, fruity wine.	Pour wine over the back of a spoon to create a float.

> "The water was not fit to drink. To make it palatable, we had to add whiskey. By diligent effort, I learned to like it"
> Sir Winston Churchill

Pink Rabbit

In 1948, Nestle developed a chocolate powder mix that easily turned milk into chocolate milk. In the US, it was called Nestle Quik. In 1973, the Nestle Quik Bunny, named Quiky, was introduced as the company's mascot in the US.

By year 2000, the powder was renamed Nesquik, and Quiky took over as mascot worldwide. The "Q" on his chest was changed to an "N", and Nestle changed his name to "Nesquik Bunny". Quiky appeared in several television commercials, and many featured the recognizable jingle: "It's so rich and thick and choco-lick! But you can't drink it slow if it's Quik!" Nestle introduced the Strawberry flavor in 1960.

Recipe

Craig Nelson of Proof created this adult throwback to the Quik rabbit of our youth, with a sweet and spicy summertime refresher.

1 oz. Hendrick's gin
1 oz. Ancho Reyes liqueur
3 oz. Strawberry milk
3 dashes mole bitters

Strawberry Milk:
Whole milk
Strawberry preserves
Vanilla Bean

Shake all ingredients with ice and strain into a chilled wine glass filled with ice. Garnish with strawberry and a mint sprig.

Strawberry Milk:
Steep 1 cup whole milk, 2 tablespoons of strawberry preserves, and scraped vanilla bean in the refrigerator overnight. Strain.

{ *"The Greek word for "return" is nostos. Algos means "suffering." So nostalgia is the suffering caused by an unappeased yearning to return."*
Milan Kundera, Ignorance }

The Fairgrounds

Scots, Irish, and other Europeans who settled and farmed the American South during the late 1700s and early 1800s brought knowledge of distilling with them from the old countries. Corn was a robust, reliable, and sugar-rich crop abundant in the New World. So what did many of these bright-eyed, thirsty folks do? They started making whiskey using old world techniques and new world mash. (And by the way, a few names from among these early entrepreneurs? Try Jacob Beam, Elijah Craig, and Evan Williams. Oh yeah.)

From 1920 to 1933, Prohibition ruined many bourbon distilleries. Some of the majors came back online once the country realized its awful mistake and repealed the goddamn 18th Amendment, but it would not be until the late 20th century that bourbon saw a true resurgence, with craft distilleries and new small-batch runs from the majors popping up.

Recipe

With a history as a former 19th-century cotton mill and cigar factory, Downtown Charleston's Bar Mash space alone makes you want to guzzle down some of the American whiskey and beer bar's extensive bourbon collection.

1 oz. Woodford Reserve Double Oak bourbon
1 oz. clarified apple juice
½ oz. Pedro Ximénez sherry
½ oz. Cardamaro liquer
2 dashes Angostura bitters
1 dash Bitterman's Elemakule Tiki bitters
1 oz. saline

Pour the ingredients into a mixing glass and pour over the rocks. Express an orange peel and rub along the rim.

{ *"I wish to live to 150 years old, but the day I die, I wish it to be with a cigarette in one hand and a glass of whiskey in the other."*
Ava Gardner }

Harvey Wallbanger

The Harvey Wallbanger has **one** of the most memorable names in cocktail history. Donato "Duke" Antone, the largely forgotten bartender who, according to longstanding legend, is the creator of the Wallbanger, as well as a number other two-ingredient wonders of the time, like the Rusty Nail and White Russian. Antone ran Duke's "Blackwatch" Bar on Sunset Boulevard in Hollywood in the 1950s. According to folklore, Donato invented the Harvey Wallbanger in 1952. It is said he named it after a Manhattan Beach surfer and regular named Tom Harvey. But the cocktail didn't become popular until the early 1970s. This sudden reversal of fortunes coincides with the arrival of George Bednar, who in 1966 became marketing director of McKesson Imports Co., an importing company that handled Galliano. Previously, the liqueur had a staid ad campaign that featured the line "Fond of things Italiano? Try a sip of Galliano." Bednar somehow found the Wallbanger and hoisted it up the barroom flagpole. The original ads pushed the drink as a replacement at brunch for the Bloody Mary. Round about late 1969, a rather pained-looking, sandal-wearing mascot named Harvey Wallbanger appeared. His line: "Harvey Wallbanger is the name and I can be made!"

Recipe

The Thoroughbred Club, located in the lobby of the Charleston Place Hotel, lives up to every hotel bar stereotype with an affected, dark-hued space settled with red leather seating and framed equestrian memorabilia.

1 ½ oz. vodka	Pour the vodka and orange juice into a collins glass with ice cubes.
4 ounces orange juice	
½ oz. Galliano L'Autentico	Layer the Galliano on top by pouring it slowly over the back of a bar spoon.
Orange slice and cherry for garnish	Garnish with an orange slice and maraschino cherry.

{ *By 1981, Duke had opened a new academy, Antone's School of Mixology, and was full-on boasting that he was the genesis of "the Harvey Wallbanger, the Rusty Nail, the White Russian and the Kamakazi, as well as the Freddie Fudpucker."* }

Red Wedding

Recipe

This modern warehouse/barnhouse/beer hall hybrid tucked inconspicuously amongst the no-man's land that demarks North Charleston from the Peninsula, Edmund's Oast serves New American fare, beer brewed on-site and craft cocktails. Cult-ish domestic crafts like Coast, Evil Twin, and Prairie Artisan Ales are posted next to hard-to-find imports (De Struise, Nøgne ø, J.W. Lees...), all available alongside house-made jerky, charcuterie, and other indulgent bar snacks.

Red Wedding Ice Cubes:
3 cups boiling water
¼ cup loose-leaf hibiscus tea
½ cup brewed English Breakfast tea
6 thyme sprigs
¼ teaspoon orange blossom water
¾ cup Demerara sugar
¾ cup ginger ale, preferably Blenheim's

Cocktail:
Orange peel
½ oz. Averna
2 oz. aged bourbon, preferably Elijah Craig 12-year-old bourbon
3 Red Wedding ice cubes (recipe above)

1. Make the ice cubes: In a large heatproof bowl, combine the water, hibiscus tea, English breakfast tea, thyme and orange blossom water and let steep for 5 minutes. Add the sugar and stir until dissolved. Add the ginger ale, then strain through a fine mesh strainer into a pitcher. Pour into 1-inch square ice cube molds and freeze until solid.

2. Make the cocktail: In a double Old Fashioned glass, muddle the orange peel with the Averna. Add bourbon and stir briefly, then add ice cubes and stir until just chilled, about 20 seconds. Serve immediately.

{ *"A lady came up to me one day and said 'Sir! You are drunk', to which I replied 'I am drunk today madam, and tomorrow I shall be sober but you will still be ugly."*
Winston S. Churchill }

Charleston Fruit Tea

It is such a simple idea, so plainly obvious that many Southerners can't believe they didn't think of it first: take the South's trademark refreshment — sweet iced tea — and make it alcoholic.

That, essentially, was the recipe used in 2008 by Irvin-House vineyards and their Firefly distillery to create a phenomenon. Its elixir, Firefly Sweet Tea Vodka, tastes almost exactly like the beloved sweet tea poured at generations of Southern family reunions, church meetings and picnics. For Firefly Distillery, the South is a source not only of inspiration but ingredients. The vodka is distilled, in part, from wine of muscadine grapes, native to Southern states. Some of the tea that is infused in the vodka, after sugar is baked into the leaves, is grown on the Charleston Tea Plantation, about five miles from the distillery.

Recipe

39 Rue de Jean looks like it's been at 39 John St. forever and in Upper King's recent restaurant history, it has. For the past 16 years the brasserie has kept regulars returning thanks to French classics and then some.

1½ oz. Firefly Sweet Tea Vodka
½ oz. Cassis or raspberry puree
Sour mix

Pour a generous portion of vodka and cassis into a shake with ice. Finish with sour mix. Shake, and strain over rocks into a tall glass, garnished with a lemon.

{ *"Anything that comes out of the South is going to be called grotesque by the northern reader, unless it is grotesque, in which case it is going to be called realistic."*
Flannery O'Connor }

CHARLESTON'S
Breweries

It's one thing to be able to lay claim to outstanding bars and restaurants, expertly crafting a host of delicious libations. But Charleston isn't just a pretty face; she has some serious chops in brewing a host of beers, with several attracting a regional and even national following

COAST
1250 N 2nd St.

Jaime Tenny and David Merritt opened COAST in a repurposed Navy record storage building in North Charleston in 2007.

FREEHOUSE
2895 Pringle St.

Set idyllically on the banks of the Ashley River, Arthur Lucas's Freehouse Brewery uses organic ingredients to produce locally unique styles.

FROTHY BEARD
225 Meeting St.

The three beards behind Frothy Beard opened their whimsically-themed nanobrewery in North Charleston in 2012, with ever-changing brews.

HOLY CITY
4155 Dorchester Rd.

Four friends opened HCB in the summer of 2011, re-purposing an old warehouse space into a GABF medal-winning destination.

LOW TIDE
2863 Maybank Hwy.

Johns Island first brewery, opened in 2016 by Owner/COO Mike Fielding and Head Brewer Andy Elliott.

PALMETTO
289 Huger St.

Built in 1993 as the first brewery to open in South Carolina after Prohibition, Palmetto blazed the trail for 14 years before another brewery opened.

REVELRY
10 Conroy St.

Only the second brewery to open in downtown proper, Revelry's first entries in the U.S. Beer Open Championships netted them four medals.

TRADESMAN
1639 Tatum St.

James Island's first brewery opened in 2014, the brainchild of Scott McConnell and his wife Sara Gayle. Their aim is true: to brew great beer for the common man.

WESTBROOK
510 Ridge Rd, Mt. P

Edward and Morgan Westbrook opened Mount Pleasant's first brewery in late 2010, Their IPA and White Thai, are available year-round, and are area favorites

Jammer Juice

In the tropics themselves, as Jeff Berry writes in his introduction to <u>Potions of the Caribbean</u>, "Rum mixed with sugar and lime made the nasty, brutish, short life of the average Caribbean combatant worth living." Despite movie franchises such as Pirates of the Caribbean depicting Caribbean cutthroats swigging straight from bottles of rum, such 17th and 18th century ruffians preferred a bowl of rum punch. There are countless tales of merchant seamen being lured with punch only to find themselves surrounded by pirates. Indeed, it was the infamous Captain Kidd who negotiated a privateer contract over rum punch with the then commander-in-chief of England's Caribbean forces.

Recipe

For decades, The Windjammer has been a destination for tourists, locals, beach bums, and young music fans. The long bar slings a lot of different cocktails and beers. The summer season brings the weekly Bikini Bash competition and volleyball tournaments.

1½ oz. Captain Morgan's Spiced Rum
1½ oz. cranberry juice
1½ oz. orange juice
1½ oz. pineapple juice

Add liquid ingredients to a cocktail shaker and fill with ice. Shake to perfection and enjoy on the porch watching beach volleyball.

{ *Popular belief has it that name 'punch' originates from the Hindi word for 'five', a reference to the traditional number of ingredients: sour (lime or lemon), sugar, spirit (rum, brandy or arrack), water and spice (nutmeg).* }

Air Mail

Though not fully official on account of the plane breaking down, the first attempt at modern airmail was documented in 1911. It traveled from Petaluma to Santa Rosa, California and contained exactly three pieces of correspondence. The first instance of the Air Mail cocktail was documented in Esquire magazine's 1949 edition of Handbook for Hosts. It's not certain why the drink is named for the modern delivery method, but it can be said the Air Mail is quite like the Caribbean version of a French 75, with a splash of lime whisked into a turbulent mix of rum, honey and Champagne. Fast forward to 2015, when Douglas Ford pens an excellent piece on the Air Mail, claiming that it actually came from a 1930's Bacardi promotional pamphlet published in Cuba. He added that the date and time rationally explains the cocktail's name, since Cuba had just added an air mail system in 1930.

Recipe

The Ordinary, located in a 1927 limestone-and-brick bank building, looks much the same on the outside, but its interior has been restored to its original open and impressive proportions, starring a ceiling that's approximately 23 feet high. The bank is one of the best small surviving works by Simons and Lapham Architects, downtown Charleston's most prolific firm in the 1920s and 1930s.

1½ oz. añejo rum
¾ oz. fresh lime juice
1 oz. honey syrup (1:1)
1 oz. sparkling rose', chilled

Combine the rum, lime juice, syrup and ice in shaker. Shake vigorously. Strain into a chilled glass and top with sparkling rose'. Garnish by dragging mint leaf through bitters to create an attractive design, then laying mint leaf on top.

{ *"Don't talk to me about Naval tradition! It's nothing but rum, sodomy, and the lash"*
Winston Churchill }

The Warthog

Gin gets its name from the Dutch word for juniper, which is genever, and the root of the English slander "Dutch Courage". Gin likely traces its origins to liquors produced back in the Middle Ages, with references to a spirit flavored with "genever" referenced in a 13th Century Flemish manuscript. By the 1600s, the Dutch were producing gin in earnest, with hundreds of distilleries in the city of Amsterdam alone.In the latter half of the 17th Century and in the early years of the 18th Century, gin rapidly gained popularity in England, cementing the association it still enjoys with that nation. In fact, by the year 1720, some experts estimate that as many as a quarter of the households in London frequently produced their own gin. The period in the storied city's history became known as "The Gin Craze," an era that was so awesome Parliament had to pass no fewer than five major legislative acts over the course of 22 years in a vain attempt to rein in the population's consumption of gin.

Recipe

A nod to the classic 1920's speakeasy, Prohibition feels like you're stepping back in time with its bourbon barrel ceiling and vintage inspired decor. Our cocktails and cuisine, however, are anything but old-fashioned. Begin with an inventive cocktail crafted by Beverage Director Jim McCourt, who constantly dreams up balanced and thought-provoking libations.

2 oz. Striped Pig Gin
¾ oz. St. George Spiced Pear
¾ oz. lemon juice
¾ oz. honey sauce

Add ingredients to a cocktail shaker with ice and shake vigorously. Pour into a martini glass and garnish with a roasted rosemary sprig.

{ *. "I exercise strong self-control. I never drink anything stronger than gin before breakfast."*
W.C. Fields }

Broad Street Barrister

The term "Blind Tiger" was coined in the late 1800's to describe the illicit drinking and gambling establishments opening their doors as temperance legislation swept across the country. The first "Blind Tigers" in South Carolina sprung up in the Holy City in 1893 as a defiant rebuttal to the "Dispensary" laws mandated by the infamous Governor Ben "Pitchfork" Tillman.

Local lore suggests Broad Street was home to many houses of "ill repute" throughout the years. In 1992, ninety-nine years after the first "Blind Tigers" appeared, the "Blind Tiger Pub" opened in its current location, paying homage to a historic tradition. Given it's proximity to the "Law Corner", this aptly named cocktail serves the thirsty attorneys and tourists alike.

Recipe

Housed in a building constructed in 1803, the Blind Tiger was a home away from home since it first opened its doors in the late eighties. From the beginning, the pub was a place where the people of Charleston could take a break from the realities of the lives. From college, from work, from their families. Imagine St. Elmo's meets Cheers, and there you have it, the Blind Tiger Pub.

1½ oz. Virgil Kane whiskey
1 sugar cube
1 orange peel
3 dashes Fee Brothers orange bitters
3 dashes Angostura bitters

Place sugar cube in old fashioned glass and saturate with bitters, add a dash of plain water. Muddle until dissolved. Fill the glass with ice cubes and add whiskey. Garnish with orange slice, and a cocktail cherry.

{ *"Why don't they pass a constitutional amendment prohibiting anybody from learning anything? If it works as well as prohibition did, in five years Americans would be the smartest race of people on Earth."*
Will Rogers }

Broad Steet, Charleston around 1910

Charleston was not known for its strict adherance
to the 18th Amendment.

That's My Jam

The history of cachaça actually begins with the history of Brazil itself. Around 1530, the Portuguese began to colonize what is now the northeastern part of the country using a plantation method similar to the ones employed in the Caribbean and southern regions of the United States. Sugarcane production appeared as the first major exploration venture, since the Portuguese had already mastered the planting and processing in the Madeira Islands.

In the sugar manufacturing process, slaves performed the sugarcane harvest and proceeded to crush the stems. This crushed mass was then boiled into a thick broth until it turned into molasses. The residue of the this boiling process, was an even thicker broth, called cagaça, which was commonly fed to the animals along with other remains of sugarcane. Due to exposure to the hot climate, the cagaça would often begin to ferment in the troughs, producing a fermented liquid of high alcohol content. As strange as this may sound, the pigs and the cattle were the first ones to actually enjoy the original Brazilian cachaça.

Recipe

Another Allison Radecker from O-Ku creation, this spicy and extremely flavorful marriage of Mexican and Brazilian liquors will take you around the world.

¾ oz. Cachaça
¾ oz. blanco tequila
½ oz. lime juice
1 oz. ginger syrup
½ oz.red pepper jam, thinned

Pour the ingredients into a mixing glass filled with ice cubes. Shake well. Strain into a martini glass, rimmed with red sea salt.

{ *"Always do sober what you said you'd do drunk. That will teach you to keep your mouth shut."*
Ernest Hemingway }

Red Scare

The area off East Bay Street once formed the eastern edge of Charleston, with the wharfs located where the railroads are now. Near what was once called the Wilmington Railroad Depot, the area was heavily shelled and many buildings were violently destroyed in an 1864 Civil War explosion. As confederate soldiers planned to evacuate Charleston on February 18, they loaded the depot with weapons and supplies to ensure nothing was left for the descending Union soldiers. Despite their best efforts, a storehouse on the grounds of the depot was filled with gunpowder and set on fire. A trail of gunpowder led to the Wilmington Depot, where over 200 civilians still inside were killed.

Recipe

Zero George Restaurant + Bar is a hidden gem off upper East Bay, mixing some seriously heavyweight cocktails. The Red Scare is one of the most popular.

2 oz. Espolon blanco tequila
½ oz. PAMA liqueur
½ oz. Jack Rudy grenadine
¾ oz. fresh orange juice
½ oz.habanero simple syrup,
4-5 cilantro leaves

Add liquid ingredients to a cocktail shaker with ice and shake it like a Polaroid picture. Double strain into a martini glass and express lime around the rim. Top with cilantro micro-greens. You want the drink to still be laughing at you!

{ *"It takes only one drink to get me drunk. The trouble is, I can't remember if it's the thirteenth or the fourteenth."*
George Burns }

S.S. Pepper

As with so many popular things, more than one person has claimed to have invented the margarita. One of the most prevalent stories is that Carlos "Danny" Herrera developed the drink at his Tijuana-area restaurant, Rancho La Gloria, around 1938. As the legend goes, Herrera dreamed up the cocktail for one of his customers, an aspiring actress named Marjorie King who was allergic to all hard alcohol other than tequila. To make the liquor more palatable to his fussy client, he combined the elements of a traditional tequila shot—a lick of salt and a wedge of lime—and turned them into a refreshing drink.

Recipe

Named after a regular, Sarah Steele, who lives for spicy cocktails, this spicy garden variation of a margarita is a real crowd favorite at The MacIntosh.

1 oz Blanco Tequila
1 oz Red Bell Pepper Cordial*
¾ oz. lime juice
½ oz. Honey Syrup**
3 dashes Jalapeno Tincture***

Shake well, single strain over fresh ice

Glass: Rocks
Garnish: Healthy dollop of Salt Foam**** and microplane of lime zest

*Red Bell Pepper Cordial: equal parts fresh juiced bell pepper, simple syrup and vodka

**Honey Syrup: equal parts honey and water

***Jalapeno Tincture: infusion of freshly sliced jalapenos and a high proof neutral grain spirit (everclear)...allow to macerate for at least 1 day

***Salt foam: 1 pint of water, 2 oz salt, 2 oz lime juice, 1 bar spoon of soy lecithin. Mix with hand blender, and voila!

{ *According to The Complete Book of Spirit, the first importer of Jose Cuervo in the United States advertised with the tagline, "Margarita: it's more than a girl's name," in 1945.* }

Barn Burner

The special character of Mount Pleasant's Old Village Historic District results from the particular social history of the area, especially since 1759, when the oldest surviving house was built. In the historic district varied examples of historic architecture still stand along the community's oldest streets thanks to the residents and property owners who have preserved it. As the streetscapes illustrate, Mount Pleasant history continues. Its buildings document the growth more vividly than any records or writings can. It attests to the area's origins as an early land grant up through the modern era, but without the urban sprawl that has infected many of the state's coastal towns and cities.

Recipe

Housed in a restored 19-century general store on charming Pitt Street, the Old Village Post House now belongs in the Hall Management Group's portfolio. The Barn Burner is one of their most popular cocktails.

1½ oz. Larceny bourbon
1 oz. clarified apple juice
½ oz. Pedro Ximénez sherry
½ oz. Cardamaro amaro liquor
2 dashes Angostura bitters
1 dash Bitterman's Elemakule Tiki bitters
1 dash saline

Stir ingredients in a pint glass, and served over the rocks. Express an orange peel and run around the rim.

{
"I like to have a martini,
Two at the very most.
After three I'm under the table,
after four I'm under my host."
Dorothy Parker
}

39

Charleston Cocktail

At one point in our nation's history, Madeira was not just a favorite wine, but the main wine of its time. What's more, it was one of the primary imported goods for ports such as Savannah and Charleston and a great source of wealth in the colonies. Indeed, it was so favored that Madeira was the wine with which the Declaration of Independence and the inauguration of George Washington both were toasted. It played a key role in stoking revolutionary feelings against the British in Boston when one of John Hancock's ships carrying Madeira was delayed from entering port by British customs agents—it was the wine beloved by our Founding Fathers. Ships carrying the wine came from Portugal—Madeira is an archipelago belonging to Portugal—and first call was at Boston, then New York, and so on down the eastern coast until finally reaching the port of Charleston

Recipe

High Cotton opened in 1999 as a brassy Southern steakhouse, full of brick and leather, but delicate in the way it looked out upon the town. High Cotton and Maverick Southern Kitchens' other flagship, Slightly North of Broad, anchor the end of a street that made Charleston the envy of Southern food towns.

1½ oz. vodka
1½ oz. Sercial Madeira, such as Blandy's
2 oz. chilled brewed black tea
1 oz. fresh lemon juice
½ oz. simple syrup
½ oz. mint syrup
½ oz. water
1 mint sprig

Fill a cocktail shaker with ice cubes. Add all of the remaining ingredients except the crushed ice and mint sprig. Shake well; strain into a pilsner glass filled with crushed ice. Garnish with the mint sprig.

{ *"We were not a hugging people. In terms of emotional comfort it was our belief that no amount of physical contact could match the healing powers of a well made cocktail."*
David Sedaris, Naked }

Employees Only

Although there is some dispute, most sources point to Don Pedro Sánchez de Tagle, the Marquis of Altamira, as the first person to mass produce tequila, beginning about 1600. However, it was not until 1795 that Don José Maria Guadalupe de Cuervo was the first to receive a license to make it from King Ferdinand IV of Spain. Don Cenobio Sauza was the first to export to tequila to the United States in 1873 when he shipped 3 barrels of it to El Paso, Texas. This was soon followed by a shipment from Don Cuervo as well.

Tequila became much more popular in the US during World War II, when importing whiskey from Europe became very difficult. Today, many credit Jimmy Buffet and his song "Margaritaville" with ensuring tequila's place in the pantheon of America's most beloved spirits.

Recipe

This industrial-chic bar Warehouse garners lines with artisanal cocktails and New American cuisine served in a dark-hued space made edgy with exposed brick. The bar serves plenty of wine and cocktails (as represented by a sleekly designed menu), but PBR and a pool table also caters adequately to the casual post-work crowd.

2 oz. green jalepeno tequila
1 oz. pink grapefruit juice
2 lime wedges, juiced
¼ oz. hibiscus blossom syrup

Mascerate one green jalapeno into a bottle of white tequila, for several days. Combine all the ingredients and shake well with ice. Strain and finish with soda; garnish with candied hibiscus blossoms.

{ *"Tequila is not even a drink; it's a way for having the cops around without using a phone."*
Dylan Moran }

Low Tide

A group of people celebrating the New Year in New Zealand built their own tiny private structure in coastal waters to avoid an island-wide liquor ban that was in effect during New Year's events.

The group of "Kiwis" built the sand structure during low tide on a Sunday off the coast Tairua, a town on New Zealand's northern island, according to local news, and then waited for the rising tide to surround them.

The Sydney Morning Herald tweeted a picture of the man-made alcohol island and reported that members of the group joked that they were in "international waters" and thus free from the alcohol ban that extended to beaches and outdoor events. The inhabitants of the island in the Tairua estuary rang in the 2018 New Year with alcoholic beverages.

Recipe

The Grocery, a Cannonborough eatery that evokes memories of an old-school small town grocery serving foods from local farmers and fishermen. The restaurant also has an in-house canning program to preserve fresh produce, and an excellent cocktail program features ingredients as rich in quality as the dishes.

1½ oz. Cardinal gin
¼ oz. rosemary simple syrup
½ oz. tonic water
½ oz. fresh lime juice
¾ oz. Ancho Reyes

Pour the ingredients into a mixing glass, and gently stir. Serve over crushed ice in a glass with a salt rim and a lime.

{ *"Only when the tide goes out do you discover who's been swimming naked."*
Warren Buffett }

Irish Good-Bye

One of the world's most favorite mixed drinks, the piña colada, was born in Puerto Rico, but the identity of the bartender who first mixed up the iconic rum-based cocktail remains a point of contention. The Caribe Hilton, one of the premier luxury hotels in the Puerto Rican capital of San Juan, claims the piña colada was first served up in its Beachcombers Bar in 1954 by bartender Ramon "Monchito" Marrero. Asked by hotel management to create a signature drink that captured the flavors of the island, Marrero reportedly spent three months experimenting with hundreds of combinations before perfecting his sweet, frothy concoction of rum, cream of coconut and pineapple juice. According to the Caribe Hilton, Marrero mixed up and served his creation at the hotel for 35 years until his retirement in 1989.

Recipe

Locals, a literal hole-in-the-wall bar and restaurant off Anna Knapp north of 17, punches above it's weight with food-truck quality gourmet tacos (Korean BBQ or Jerk Chicken, anyone?) and award-winning sushi, but it is the highly original take on the piña colada that blows the mind.

2 oz. banana-infused
Jameson Irish Whiskey
¾ oz. pineapple juice
½ oz. cream of coconut
¼ oz. lime juice
nutmeg, cinnamon, sugar

Add liquid ingredients to a cocktail shaker and shake vigorously. Pour over rocks, and garnish with spices and a pineapple leaf.

Banana-infused Jameson:
Sous vide three sliced overripe bananas and a bottle of Jamesons at 150 degrees for an hour. Strain and chill.

{ *After tasting one of the hotel's piña coladas, Hollywood legend Joan Crawford reportedly declared it was "better than slapping Bette Davis in the face."* }

43

New Old-Fashioned

The earliest recorded definition of the term "cocktail," as it appeared in the periodical The Balance, and Columbian Repository in 1806, refers to the mixed drink as "a stimulating liquor, composed of spirits of any kind, sugar, water and bitters"—essentially an Old Fashioned with any spirit of your choosing. The esteemed Mr. Boston Official Bartender's Guide suggests that it was most commonly made with whiskey in the early days, so when bartenders began experimenting with new-fangled ingredients, curmudgeonly drinkers began requesting the drink in the "old-fashioned style," made simply with whiskey. In a 2016 poll of bartenders at the 100 top bars in the country, Drinks International determined the Old Fashioned reigned supreme above all other mixed drinks as the most popular order.

Recipe

When the original Cocktail, notably with a capital "C", was created, it was a noble communion of spirit, sugar, water, and bitters. If this combination sounds a lot like an Old Fashioned, you would be right because that is exactly what it is. The standard has always been whiskey, but in today's creative cocktail community, the spirit, the sugar component, and the bitters choice are up for grabs. This is the venerated Hank's take on it.

1½ oz. Bulleit bourbon
½ oz. Antica Formula vermouth
brandied cherries
muddled orange peel

Muddle an orange peel in a shaker. Add bourbon and vermouth and ice, and shake vigorously. Pour into a double old fashioned glass and top with brandied cherries.

{ *"The only way to keep your health is to eat what you don't want, drink what you don't like, and do what you'd rather not."*
Mark Twain }

CHARLESTON'S
Distilleries

The artisan, farm-to-table spirit has deep roots in the South and is now seen in Charleston's-own distillery market. Distilleries throughout the area are delighting customers with batches of fine whiskey, vodka and gin. Strong ties with neighboring farms ensure local ingredients are used to produce specialty spirits from local grains.

CHARLESTON DISTILLING

501 King St.
....

The ingredients are all the Carolina-grown corn, rye, wheat, and millet we can get our hands on. All of our grains are milled on-site in our own Millhouse at Flowers Farm in Summerton, South Carolina, then delivered to our King Street Distillery in the heart of downtown.

FIREFLY DISTILLERY

6775 Bears Bluff Rd.
....

The largest distillery in the state, Firefly Distillery offers one-of-a-kind products to go with a one-of-a-kind atmosphere. According to one of the founders, they chose "Firefly" for their name because fireflies are "magical", and bring that feeling of Southern nostalgia.

HIGH WIRE

652 King St.
....

Founded by husband and wife team, Scott Blackwell and Ann Marshall, High Wire was born of a desire to introduce small batch, handmade, craft spirits to South Carolina.All of the products are batch distilled in a hand-hammered, German copper still.

RED HARBOR RUM

No public tours
....

Justin Buchanan and Jake MacDowell dug deep into American history to create Red Harbor Rum. To design the label, fonts were taken from colonial currency, the bottle is of a 1700's mullet bottle discovered in Charleston Harbor, and the stamp on the front of the bottle incorporated a nod to the Stamp Act of 1765.

STRIPED PIG DISTILLERY

2225 Old School Dr.
....

Charleston's first post-Prohibition distiller, Striped Pig has a focus on spirits that work well in cocktails and keeping everything as locally sourced as possible...molasses from Savannah is the only non-South Carolina product they use.

VIRGIL KAINE

No public tours
....

Founded by two accomplished chefs, David Szlam and Ryan Meany were inspired to boldly blend, infuse and tinker with choice ingredients to craft rebellious whiskeys. These catergory-shattering spirits, regardless of what the industry expects, are just damn tasty.

45

The Gail

Though the Filson Historical Society is home to bourbon labels printed as early as the 1850s, he says, "the story that the name 'bourbon' comes from Bourbon County doesn't even start appearing in print until the 1870s." Instead, some believe the name evolved in New Orleans after two men known as the Tarascon brothers arrived to Louisville from south of Cognac, France, and began shipping local whiskey down the Ohio River to Louisiana's bustling port city. In the 19th century, New Orleans entertainment district was Bourbon Street, as it is today. "People starting asking for 'that whiskey they sell on Bourbon Street,'" Author Mike Veach says, "which eventually became 'that bourbon whiskey.'" Still, Veach concedes, "We may never know who actually invented bourbon, or even who the first Kentucky distiller was."

Recipe

Top Chef judge Gail Simmons spent time in Charleston filming the show, making cocktails, sipping on them, and of course, picking up a chainsaw with Joe. Here's her latest episode of Gail's Culinary Adventures at The Gin Joint.

2 oz. bourbon (We recommend Old Grand-Dad. If it was Harry Truman's bourbon of choice, it's good enough for us, too.)
¾ oz. Tippleman's Ginger Honey Syrup
¾ oz. fresh lemon juice
Handful of sage, muddled
lemon twist

Muddle lemon peel in a shaker. Add the sage, bourbon, honey syrup and lemon juice, along with ice. Shake and strain into a martini glass. Garnish with sage.

{ *"Always carry a flagon of whiskey in case of snakebite, and furthermore, always carry a small snake."*
W. C. Fields }

Cucumber my Honey

The remarkable spread of the chili (or chilli, or chile, or chile pepper, to use just a few of its myriad names and spellings) is a piquant chapter in the story of globalization. Few other foods have been taken up by so many people in so many places so quickly. Ask a Chinese chili lover or an Indian or a Thai and most will swear that chilies are native to their homeland, so integral is the spice to their cooking, so deeply embedded is it in their culture. European and American chili addicts, though less numerous, are just as passionate about the spice.The use of the Jalapeno dates back as far as the Aztecs, who were known to smoke the chiles. The Jalapeno is one of the most commonly grown chiles in Mexico, and today it is one of the most commonly used and grown in the US as well. The name is taken from the term Jalapa, which is the capital of Veracruz, Mexico.

Recipe

HōM's Gabriela Acosta claims this popular libation's addition of jalapeño honey syrup is what shocks people who try it, and consequently why they fall in love with it.

1½ Hendricks Gin
3 cucumber slices
½ oz. jalapeño honey syrup
½ oz. lime juice

jalapeño honey syrup:
2 cups honey
2 jalapeño peppers
½ cup water

Muddle the cucumbers in a shaker with the jalapeño honey syrup. Add ice, gin, and lime juice. Shake vigorously and strain over ice in a rocks glass. Garnish with a cucumber slice.

{ *"An intelligent man is sometimes forced to be drunk to spend time with his fools."*
Ernest Hemingway }

Last Word

Luxardo is a family-owned company founded in Zara, a port city on the Dalmatian coast of what is now Croatia. Girolamo Luxardo, a Genovese businessman, and his wife, Maria Canevari, moved to Zara in 1817. It was Maria who began perfecting "rosolio maraschino," a liqueur produced in Dalmatian convents since medieval times from special maraschino cherries. Canevari's liqueur was of such high quality that it gained the attention of connoisseurs, and her husband founded the Luxardo Distillery in 1821 to produce her original Maraschino. Not long afterwards, the Emperor of Austria awarded the Luxardo liqueur the highest honor "Privilegiata Fabbrica Maraschino Excelsior.". Only one member of the fourth generation, Giorgio Luxardo, survived the World War II invasion and fled to Italy. Escaping with only a cherry sapling, Giorgio crossed the Adriatic Sea to the Veneto region of northeast Italy and reconnected with a colleague who had saved the Luxardo recipe book. Armed with the surviving tools and a desire to reestablish his family's legacy, Giorgio chose the small Veneto city of Torreglia to rebuild the distillery in 1946. Today, Luxardo is operated by Franco Luxardo of the family's fifth generation, along with members of the sixth.

Recipe

Fittingly, with Star's Rooftop offering a stellar view of the city, we conclude this humble tome with the Last Word...delicious.

1½ oz. Nolet's Gin
½ oz. Luxardo cherry liquor
¾ oz. fresh lemon juice
¾ oz. chartreuese cream

Pour the ingredients into a mixing glass filled with ice cubes. Shake well. Strain into a martini glass. Serve with a twist of lime.

{ *"Frankly, I was horrified by life, at what a man had to do simply in order to eat, sleep, and keep himself clothed. So I stayed in bed and drank. When you drank the world was still out there, but for the moment it didn't have you by the throat."*
Charles Bukowski }

www.ingramcontent.com/pod-product-compliance
Lightning Source LLC
Chambersburg PA
CBHW031530040426
42445CB00009B/472